SQUADRONS!

No. 45

The Supermarine

SPITFIRE MK. IX
- THE BELGIAN & DUTCH SQUADRONS -

Phil H. LISTEMANN

ISBN: 979-1096490-74-5

Copyright

© **2021 Philedition - Phil Listemann**

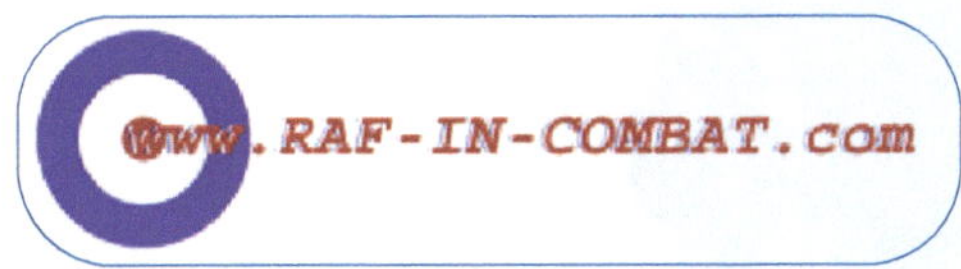

Colour profiles: Gaetan Marie/Bravo Bravo Aviation

GLOSSARY OF TERMS

PERSONEL :

(AUS)/RAF: Australian serving in the RAF
(BEL)/RAF: Belgian serving in the RAF
(CAN)/RAF: Canadian serving in the RAF
(CZ)/RAF: Czechoslovak serving in the RAF
(NFL)/RAF: Newfoundlander serving in the RAF
(NL)/RAF: Dutch serving in the RAF
(NZ)/RAF: New Zealander serving in the RAF
(POL)/RAF: Pole serving in the RAF
(RHO)/RAF: Rhodesian serving in the RAF
(SA)/RAF: South African serving in the RAF
(US)/RAF - RCAF : American serving in the RAF or RCAF

RANKS

G/C : Group Captain
W/C : Wing Commander
S/L : Squadron Leader
F/L : Flight Lieutenant
F/O : Flying Officer
P/O : Pilot Officer
W/O : Warrant Officer
F/Sgt : Flight Sergeant
Sgt : Sergeant
Cpl : Corporal
LAC : Leading Aircraftman

OTHER

ATA: Air Transport Auxiliary
CO : Commander
DFC : Distinguished Flying Cross
DFM : Distinguished Flying Medal
DSO : Distinguished Service Order
Eva. : Evaded
ORB : Operational Record Book
OTU : Operational Training Unit
PoW : Prisoner of War
PAF: Polish Air Force
RAF : Royal Air Force
RAAF : Royal Australian Air Force
RCAF : Royal Canadian Air Force
RNZAF : Royal New Zealand Air Force
SAAF : South African Air Force
s/d: Shot down
Sqn : Squadron
† : Killed

CODENAMES - OFFENSIVE OPERATIONS - FIGHTER COMMAND

CIRCUS:
Bombers heavily escorted by fighters, the purpose being to bring enemy fighters into combat.

RAMROD:
Bombers escorted by fighters, the primary aim being to destroy a target.

RANGER:
Large formation freelance intrusion over enemy territory with aim of wearing down enemy figthers.

RHUBARD:
Freelance fighter sortie against targets of opportunity.

ROADSTEAD:
Dive bombing and low level attacks on enemy ships at sea or in harbour

RODEO:
A fighter sweep without bombers.

SWEEP:
An offensive flight by fighters designed to draw up and clear the enemy from the sky.

THE SUPERMARINE SPITFIRE MK. IX

The Spitfire Mk.IX is one of the best known versions of the Spitfire. However, it should never really have existed. Its creation can be attributed to the appearance of the Focke-Wulf Fw190 over western Europe at the end of 1941. Royal Air Force pilots were quick to state the Spitfire Mk.V, the frontline RAF fighter at the time in Great Britain, was outclassed in many aspects by the new German fighter. The RAF, therefore, had to urgently find a solution to improve the Spitfire. Supermarine installed a Merlin 61, which was undergoing trials at the time, in a Mk.V airframe in order to boost its performance. The Merlin 61 was more powerful than previous engines and, coupled with a four-blade propeller and other aerodynamic refinements, it gave the Spitfire what the Mk.V needed to take on the Fw190. The results were such that the RAF attributed the Mk.IX denomination to this new version and introduced it to service as quickly as possible during the course of the summer of 1942. The first Mk.IXs were made by modifying some Mk.Vs as they left the assembly lines. Despite a difficult start, the Mk.IX soon showed what it was capable of, to such an extent that, by 1944, it had become the standard RAF frontline fighter. This 'interim' version upset the order as the Mk.VIII, which was supposed to replace the Mk.V in fighter units, was in some ways sacrificed and relegated to a secondary role before finally being sent overseas, far from Great Britain, and, therefore, the limelight! The production of the Mk.IX was hampered by a lack of Rolls-Royce Merlin 61 engines, forcing Supermarine to maintain production of the Mk.V up to the end of the summer of 1943. However, from then on, production of the Mk.IX was well established. When the last Mk.IX was delivered to the RAF in June 1945, more than 5600 had left the production lines (this figure takes into account conversions carried out on later versions). Production was such that Great Britain ceded more than 1000 to the Soviets as part of the Lend Lease Act, starting at the end of 1943. The Mk.IX was produced for almost three years and the modifications made to the basic version were few. The armament was upgraded in the autumn of 1943; the four .303 machine guns, now totally obsolete, were replaced with American-made .50in calibre machine guns (Spitfires with this arrangement were known as Mk.IXEs). Various power units were later installed: R-R Merlins 63, 66 or 70 powered the impro-

BS289 in September 1942, one of the first Spitfire Vs to be converted on the assembly line to Mk.IX standard. Externally very similar to a Mk.V, the Mk.IX was a nasty surprise for the Germans. Their numbers were limited early on, however, and the RAF had to wait until late spring 1944 for the number of Mk.IXs it required.

The only major modification to the basic Mk.IX was its conversion to a fighter-bomber, with up to three bombs carried (two 250 pounders under the wings and one 500-lb bomb on the centreline). The four .303in machine guns were also replaced by two .50in weapons that had more punch against ground targets. The Mk.IX was not suited to carrying rocket projectiles though. The .50in machine guns began to be issued en masse to 2TAF in late spring 1944. Here, the aircraft of W/C A.G. Page, wing leader of 125 Wing during the Normandy campaign in the summer of 1944, is loaded with bombs and armed with two 20mm cannons and two .50in machine guns.
(CT Collection)

ved F, LF and HF variants (the latter two being more suitable for operations at low or high altitudes respectively). A few dozen were also modified to carry photographic equipment, thus enabling them to carry out tactical reconnaissance sorties, particularly in the Mediterranean.

However, by June 1945, the variant's loss rate was startling and corresponded to the major role played by the Mk.IX in the war over Europe in 1944-45. When the war came to an end in Europe, the RAF had just 2200 Mk.IXs with units or in storage. If we remove the 1100 aircraft delivered to the Soviets and the few dozen lost by the Americans in the Mediterranean, the RAF had lost approximately half of the Mk.IXs taken on charge between 1942 and 1945. This rate of loss continued in the following months as dozens of aircraft damaged by the enemy, or just worn out from months of intensive use, were simply struck off charge. After the war, the Mk.IX was deemed obsolete, especially when compared to Spitfire variants equipped with the Griffon engine and, above all, the new kings of the sky, the jet aircraft. The Mk.IX's days were numbered, but as Great Britain needed both money and to assert its influence, it decided to offer the Mk.IX for export. This choice was also dictated by the fact that the Mk.XVI, the twin of the Mk.IX with its American-made engine and, therefore, partly financed by the United States via the Lend Lease Act, was the object of specific terms of use as the engines were officially considered property of the United States government until they were paid for, something that did not happen until much later. Thus, in the first years following the end of the war, approximately 1200 Mk.IXs swapped their RAF roundels for those of other countries to whom they were sold or ceded. After 1947, the Mk.IX was rarely used, unlike the Mk.XVI. However, in total, during the Second World War more than 100 fighter units were totally or partially equipped with the Spitfire. It should be noted this version also included a post-war two-seat version, known as the Spitfire T.IX; this was a modification of several existing single-seaters, not newly built aircraft. The Soviets had the same idea and transformed a few of their Mk.IXs into two-seaters.

From July 1944, the Belgians of No. 349 Squadron flew with Ray Harries who joined the RAF when war broke out in September 1939. Upon completing his training, he was posted to No. 43 Squadron in December 1940 to fly Hurricanes. His first tour was short as, in July 1941, he was posted as a flying instructor to No. 52 OTU. He returned to operations in January 1942 as a flight commander with No. 131 (County of Kent) Squadron. During the year, he became one of the unit's best pilots and received the DFC in September. In December he was given command of No. 91 (Nigeria) Squadron, the first unit equipped with Griffon-powered Spitfires (in April 1943). More success followed and during the year he added a Bar to his DFC in May and a second Bar in September, following his promotion to wing commander in August to lead the Tangmere Wing and its two Spitfire XII squadrons. In November he was made a Companion of the DSO and his score continued to mount. His tour ended that month. In July 1944, he became wing leader of No. 135 Wing for his third tour and made his last claim, a damaged Me262, on 26 December to bring his tally to eighteen confirmed victories (three shared), two probables and six aircraft damaged (one shared). Two months later, he relinquished command of 135 Wing and held no further operational positions before the end of the war. In June 1945, he added a Bar to his DSO. Harries remained in the RAF after the war but was killed in a flying accident in a Meteor on 14 May 1950 while OC No. 92 Squadron.
He is seen here in a 349 Sqn machine shortly after his last confirmed destroyed victory, an Fw190, claimed on 25 July 1944.

THE BELGIANS AND THE DUTCH IN THE RAF

Belgium and The Netherlands entered the war in May 1940 when they were invaded by Germany. Dutch resistance ended after five days and eighteen for the Belgians. By late May 1940, the Belgians had 180 pilots and ground crew in Britain who had escaped from Belgium or France. They wanted them gathered into a Belgian unit, like the Dutch did early in June, but that request was initially denied by the British because a large injection of RAF technical personnel would have been required to make the units operational. The Belgians were quickly re-trained and sent individually to various RAF combat units. About thirty of them participated in the Battle of Britain. This arrangement remained until the middle of 1941 when it was accepted that the Belgians could have their own units. It started slowly, however, with the formation of one flight into No. 131 (County of Kent) Squadron at the end of June 1941. This flight would serve as the nucleus for No. 350 (Belgian) Squadron at the end of the year. By that time the number of Belgians was enough to man a squadron without the support of RAF technical personnel. This time taken to form the squadron can be explained by the fact that the Belgians were almost entirely dependent on escapees from Europe, rather than volunteers from elsewhere, to build up their own force. However, they also had another asset to offer the British, their huge African colony, the Belgian Congo. Early in 1942, the Belgian authorities were extremely anxious about the vulnerability of the colony. To reinforce its defences, it was decided to raise two squadrons, one patrol unit with long-range aircraft to provide protection to the convoys, and one fighter squadron, although the need for the latter unit in the colony was less pressing. For the British, however, the threat was not that big, but it was finally agreed material would be provided to form a new fighter squadron, No. 349, with available Belgian personnel and British technical bods, the latter only temporarily. After much discussion among the politicians, 349 would, in the end, be based in West Africa, where the British needed a fighter presence that could be deployed to North Africa if required, and not in the Congo. Numbers 349 and 350 Squadrons were the only Belgian fighter units in the RAF during WW2.

For the Dutch, the situation was slightly different. While they were able to form their first squadrons as early as June 1940 (Nos. 320 and 321), it must be recalled that this could only be achieved because they had spirited away material and personnel, in this case Dutch Navy personnel, from under the noses of the Germans. The Dutch Army had its own service and many of its personnel had found asylum in Britain, but, from the start, the number of trained pilots was low as The Netherlands, in May 1940, only had a small active air force. At first the British thought they would be more useful to the Dutch colonies in the East Indies where they were already operating a rather important air force, the NEIAF. However, the Dutch government in exile notified the British that new arrivals would remain to fight against the Germans. Politics slowed the process of integration in many ways, the Dutch being split between the will to fight the Germans (while the RAF needed any pilot it could get) and the need to reinforce the East Indies against the increasing Japanese threat. For the Dutch personnel in the UK who had family in Holland, the decision to be incorporated into the NEIAF was not an automatic one and they were largely reluctant to do so. In any case, the Dutch pilots had to be trained or re-trained and, when available, posted to existing RAF squadrons. There were not enough to form a full Dutch fighter unit, and no clear decision was made in 1941, so the situation remained unresolved until Java surrendered to the Japanese in March 1942. From then, the solution was simple. Some additional Dutch personnel were repatriated to Britain after that date, but they had nowhere else to go. It opened the door to the formation of a full Dutch fighter squadron. A specific Dutch unit, as with the Belgians, saw its birth as a flight within an operational unit, No. 167 (Gold Coast) Squadron, which progressively formed throughout 1942. In June 1943, a Dutch fighter squadron in the RAF was finally formed. It would be the only one.

Victories - confirmed or probable claims: 6.0 + 1 V-1

First operational sortie:
25.02.44
Last operational sortie:
27.04.45

Number of sorties: *ca.* **3,670**

Total aircraft written-off: 32

Aircraft lost on operations: 29
Aircraft lost in accidents: 3

Squadron code letters:
GE

COMMANDING OFFICERS

S/L Yvan DU MONCEAU DE B.	RAF No. 87700	(BEL)/RAF	...	21.07.44
S/L Albert VAN DE VELDE	RAF No. 123067	(BEL)/RAF	21.07.44	31.03.45
S/L Raymond LALLEMAND	RAF No. 116472	(BEL)/RAF	31.03.45	...

SQUADRON USAGE

Since its re-formation in Great Britain in June 1943, 349 Squadron, contrary to its sister squadron, No. 350, had seen limited action. In early 1944, 349 swapped its Spitfire Mk.Vs for Mk.IXs. The unit was based at Friston and commanded by S/L du Monceau. The conversion was coupled with a transfer from Air Defence of Great Britain to 83 Group of 2TAF, meaning much more action could be expected. The Mk.IXs were received in mid-February and conversion proceeded easily. The pilots continued to fly the Mk.V on operations while practicing on the Mk.IX and the last sorties on the old aircraft were carried out on the 22nd; the first on Mk.IXs three days later. Ramrod 589 was an uneventful escort for fourteen Mosquitos attacking a target near Belleville in Normandy. A Ranger was flown the next day, followed by another escort on the 29th (Ramrod 601), but, again, these proved uneventful. By the end of the month, 349 was operating MH610/Z, MJ294/X, MJ353/J, MJ369/H, MJ569/L, MJ748/A, MJ879/G,

'Duke' du Monceau de Bergendael became the top scorer of all Belgian fighter pilots in WW2, with eight comfirmed kills. He joined the Belgian military forces as a regular officer, serving first in the cavalry in 1938 before transferring to the Aéronautique Militaire one year later. He was still under training when Belgium was invaded in May 1940. He completed his training with the RAF and his first operational posting was to No. 253 Squadron in April 1941. He then served with Nos. 56 and 609 Squadrons before joining No. 350 Squadron in March 1942 as a flight commander. He eventually commanded 349 Sqn when this unit relocated to the UK, leading it for a year. He ended the war with eight confirmed victories and earned a DFC and Bar. He continued to serve in the new Belgian Air Force after the war and retired as a Major-General in 1972.
(André Bar)

Spitfire MJ294 was among the first Mk.IXs taken on charge in February 1944. This aircraft became the first Mk.IX flown by S/L du Monceau. *(André Bar)*

MJ889/W MJ962/F, MJ964/T, MK130/P, MK135/K, MK136/N, MK148/R, MK153/S, MK175/B, MK233/C, MK354/V and MK363/U. Little operational flying was performed in March, with only five days contributing sixty sorties. More importantly, the squadron moved to Hornchurch on the 11th. Early April was quiet, no ops were flown, but intensive training focussed on dive-bombing. The squadron moved to Selsey, near Portsmouth, on 11 April. The first days at Selsey were plagued by various accidents, with one crash, on the 13th, seriously damaging the Spitfire and another, following a technical failure two days later at Westhampnett, wrote off the aircraft. The pilot, F/Sgt R. Vanderbosh escaped without injury. Operations resumed on the 18th after several cancellations due to bad weather. The op involved dive-bombing a target near Abbeville with the Wing; good results were obtained. The squadron went on air cover beyond Dieppe on the 20th and followed up with a fighter sweep beyond Saint-Omer. Both were uneventful. The next day 349 returned to the Abbeville area for another dive-bombing attack. While some good results were again confirmed, the flak was accurate and F/O J. Moreau de Melen was hit in the engine. He managed to get his aircraft over the Channel, baled out twenty miles off Beachy Head, and, fortunately, was picked up by a Walrus within forty minutes. The squadron was airborne almost every day for the rest of the month, but further operational losses were sustained. On the 28th, while escorting American Marauders, F/Sgt H. Limet did not switch to the main tank before his extra tanks ran dry (probably caused by an air lock in his fuel system) and made a forced landing near the Seine river. He was taken prisoner. The next day, F/Sgt A. Moureau crashed on taking-off from Friston while returning to Selsey. He escaped injury, but his Spitfire was only good for parts salvage. In May, as the weather permitted flying without restriction, about 350 escort and dive-bombing sorties, sometimes flown from Manston, were carried out. On the 9th, the wing leader, W/C P.J. Simpson, flew with the squadron while the Wing escorted bombers attacking the Abbeville marshalling yards. No incident was reported. This was not the case the day after. During another bomber escort, targeting the Creil marshalling yards this time, F/O P. Libert experienced engine trouble and had to bale out. May 10 was not a lucky day for him as, exactly four years previously, he was badly burnt when a German bomb set fire to his Hurricane at Schaeffen in Belgium. This time the consequences were different as he was immediately taken prisoner. Despite intensive flying, no further losses were recorded until the 21st when, while attacking a ground target, F/O M. Sans was hit by flak. He managed to keep control of his machine despite the huge hole in the right wing. When he had Beachy Head in sight, and with control of the Spitfire becoming increasingly difficult, he elected to bale out over the Channel. Fortunately, he was picked up half an hour later. The same misadventure happened to F/O J. Ester, who baled out ten miles off Le Tréport, but he had to spend an hour and a half in the water before being rescued by a Walrus that then developed a leak and nearly sank on the spot. Another Walrus eventually came to the rescue. Operations continued as usual in to June until D-Day and all went well. On 6 June, the pilots woke up very early and were at readiness from 04.40. The first sortie was carried out at 05.30 with a patrol on the eastern flank of the invading forces. No enemy aircraft were seen on this sortie or the second one which took place mid-morning. A third patrol, led by F/L G. Seydel, was flown in the middle of the afternoon. A few miles north-east of Caen, F/O J. Moreau de Melen saw a Ju88 diving westward from cloud three miles south-west of Cabourg. He immediately jettisoned his bomb and went after this Ju88 with his number two, F/Sgt J. Moureau. The

No. 349 Squadron did its Air Firing Practice at Ayr in Scotland in intensely cold weather. Above, MK175/GE-B and below, MK148/GE-R. *(André Bar)*

Germans saw the two Spitfires approaching and the pilot dived to zero feet along the canal running north-east of Caen. Moreau followed in line astern, firing an ineffectual burst with cannon and machine guns from 600 yards. At the same time F/Sgt Moureau fired a short machine gun burst. The chase continued and F/O Moreau managed to open fire again with two second bursts, seeing strikes on the fuselage. The Junkers continued on and changed direction to head west again. Moreau closed in and fired a four second burst with all of his weapons, closing from 250 yards to 200 yards. Many strikes were seen on the right engine and forward part of the fuselage. A cowling and many pieces flew away, but the Junkers was still airborne and now Moreau was out of ammunition. Flight Sergeant Moureau closed in now and, from a good position, fired a two second burst with cannons and machine guns, closing from 200 to 150 yards, and hit the Junkers in the fuselage and cockpit. The Ju88 now appeared to be fatally hit as it climbed out of control to the right. Moureau followed and fired a final burst of three seconds from 30°. He broke away as the Junkers dived to the ground where it exploded ten miles west of Caen. The victory was shared by the two Belgian pilots. This Ju88 was not the only encounter as others were attacked by 349 pilots, adding further claims to the squadron's ledger. The destruction of another Ju88 was shared by two other Belgian pilots, F/Sgt J. van Melkot and Sgt J. Bragard, while four more were damaged. These were the first claims credited to 349. Flight Sergeant van Melkot did not have time to celebrate his claim, however, as, while heading for home, he received a direct flak hit in the engine. He immediately turned back towards the Allied lines but the engine stopped about thirty seconds later, smoke and flames coming out of the spinner and cowling. He made a crash-landing east of Colombelles and was eventually taken prisoner. He was released by US troops near Rennes on 4 August but never flew on operations again. Later that day a fourth sortie was carried out but proved uneventful. The next day, the 7th, started well for 349 as F/L G. Seydel managed to engage a Fw190 south-west of Caen as it diced with two other Spitfires near the town; he lodged a damaged claim as a result. Sadly, that claim was overshadowed during the following patrol of the day when F/O M. Sans was killed after being shot down by flak near Carpiquet. The next day also produced mixed results. Patrols continued over the landing beaches and, on the first one, at 06.25, Seydel, who was leading, saw some Fw190s flying eastwards and jettisoning their bombs over the sea about six miles west of Trouville. He made a 360° turn and dived to 500 feet where he found himself just behind the last Fw190 as the other pilots of the patrol took up the chase. He fired a short burst with cannons, closing from 700 to 500 yards, whereupon the Fw190 made a climbing turn to the left. He closed in again and fired two short bursts with cannons and machine guns from 200 yards, seeing strikes on the left wing and fuselage. The hood blew off and pieces fell away from the aircraft. Just behind, his number two, W/O D. Clarke, a Kiwi, had followed and began to fire at the Fw190 as well so Seydel broke away. The Fw190 was seen to dive and explode on impact with the ground. The victory was shared by the two pilots. The presence of Clarke, and several other Commonwealth flyers, was due to a temporary shortage of operational Belgian pilots. In the meantime, the other Fw190s had been engaged but the advantage swung to the Germans who managed to shoot down F/Sgt J. Gheyssens who was seen to bale out west of Dinan-sur-Mer.

Pilots of 349 Sqn at Selsey in March 1944:
Left to right, back row: Flight Sergeants G. Halleux, J. Gheyssens (†08.06.44), J. Van Molkot, H. Limet, A. Moureau, and J. Moureau, F/O Ph. Maskens, P/O H. Goldsmit (†03.11.44), and Dr. J. Degand MO.
Second row: Cpl Barnes (groundcrew - British), F/Sgt J. Groensteen (†20.04.45 with 350), Flying Officers A. Lemaire, J. Fromont, M. Siraut, P. Libert, M. Sans (†07.06.44), and J. Moreau, Sgt L. Vingerhoets (groundcrew - Belgian), and Cpl Howe (groundcrew - British).
Front row: Cpl E. Dickson (groundcrew - British), Flight Lieutenants H.W. Gulson (A&SD - British), and A. Drossaert, CO Y. du Monceau, Flight Lieutenants G. Seydel and E. Piercot, and Sgt Innes (groundcrew - British).
(André Bar)

Scenes at Selsey in February-March 1944. Above, Spitfire MJ748/GE-A having its left 20mm cannon cleaned. This aircraft has the squadron emblem painted under the exhausts, but this practice was very short-lived and not all of the Spitfires received this decoration.
Below, in the background, MK354/GE-V and, on its right, MK148/GE-R being prepared for their next flight. MJ354 was initially regularly flown by F/O J. Moreau.
(André Bar)

Some Belgian pilots posing with one of the squadron's first Spitfire IXs, complete with the squadron emblem that would be used for the future squadron crest. This emblem was short-lived and had disappeared by D-Day.

Above, on the wing: Flying Officers M. Siraut (who designed the emblem) and J. Ester. On top: F/Sgt J. Van Molkot, Flying Officers A. Lemaire and J. Moreau de Melen, F/Sgt R. Vandenbosch, and P/O H. Goldsmit (†03.11.44). In the cockpit is F/Sgt H. Limet. All but Goldsmit were veterans of the May 1940 campaign with the Belgian Army or the Belgian Aéronautique Militaire.

Below, the same group of pilots now posing aside 349's emblem: Standing: F/O M. Siraut, P/O H. Goldsmit, Flying Officers A. Lemaire, J. Moreau de Melen and J. Ester, and F/Sgt J. Van Molkot and, on top, F/Sgt R. Vandenbosch with F/Sgt H. Limet still in the cockpit.
(André Bar)

Soon after D-Day, S/L du Monceau began to regularly fly a new Spitfire IX (ML365). The letter 'I' painted on the D-Day stripes suggests the aircraft was coded GE-I, possibly referring to his first name, Ivan, the Engish variant of Yvan. *(André Bar)*

He did not survive and was killed the day of his 28 years old. During the following patrol, Fw190s were again encountered, but the German aircraft rapidly flew out of range. The third patrol of the day proved uneventful. Intensive flying occurred over the next few days but, even though the Luftwaffe remained very active in the area, nothing more than furtive encounters were recorded as far as 349 was concerned. The squadron suffered some more losses though. On the 12th, upon returning to base from a patrol, F/Sgt R. Vandenbosch collided with the Spitfire of F/O A. Oger who, after trying to follow F/O J. Fromont all over the sky over the bridgehead, had stopped short of petrol just off the runway. The rest of the month remained intense and, by its end, more than 630 sorties had been logged. The squadron then moved with the Wing to Coolham. This stay was brief as another move was made to Funtington, near Chichester, on 4 July. The moves hampered the operational tempo with 475 sorties flown for the month. The new move came with a new role: escorting Bomber Command heavy bombers or 2TAF medium bombers. Some sweeps or standing patrols were also occasionally flown. Despite this high number of sorties, no operational losses were recorded that month even though, on the 12th, a recently posted in British pilot, F/O A.A.G. Pautigny, was killed in a flying accident near Biggin Hill. He apparently failed to recover from a 45° dive for unknown reasons. A few days later a change of command took place, S/L du Monceau being at the end of his tour, with the A Flight commander, F/L A. Van der Velde, taking charge. Further changes occurred at the same time as the B Flight commander, G. Seydel, was also tour expired. The two newly promoted Flight COs were Flying Officers L. Lelarge and P. Siroux, both ex-350, who would arrive in due course. A few days later, the 26th, despite July being relatively uneventful from an operational point of view, 349 scored against the Luftwaffe. That day, 135 Wing was tasked with escorting 36 Mitchells and 24 Bostons from 2TAF to attack a dump at Alençon. About thirty German fighters tried to intercept, but the Spitfires were ready for them. The Belgians were the ones who scored the most and two confirmed victories were filed. One went to F/L Siroux and the second was claimed by F/L Seydel who was flying his final ops with 349. The latter got a Bf109 at 18,000 feet with two bursts, the first a half a second burst of cannons and machine guns from dead astern and above. He saw hits in the cockpit and right wing root before the Bf109 turned slowly on its back and went down in a vertical dive. Seydel followed the fatally damaged fighter and fired another burst of two seconds from 300 yards, seeing pieces fly away. Flight Lieutenant Seydel started to orbit and observed the Bf109 going down vertically and hitting the ground at the corner of a wood where it burst into flames. Three other pilots made claims: F/Sgt D.A. Smerdon (British), F/O A. Uydens and F/O J. Ester each claimed a damaged Bf109. No loss was recorded by the Belgians. What they did not know, however, was that these were the last claims of the war credited to the squadron; at least against aircraft as, two days later, F/O J. Moreau, returning from a bomber escort attacking Noball sites west of Lille, sighted a V-1 and shot it down north of Tonbridge.

An unusual event took place during the first week of August. On the evening of the 4th, a V-1 bomb crashed in B Flight's dispersal

D12

135 WING PERSONAL
COMBAT REPORT No. 31.

7648

A. 26th July 1944.
B. 349 Squadron
C. Spitfire IX LF
D. 09.27 - 11.10 hrs
E. 10.35.
F. Alencon area
G. 15,000 ft
H. 16,000 ft.
I. Nil.
J. 1 Me 109 destroyed.

F/LT. P.A.J.D. SIROUX.

K.   As Yellow 1 I was flying on the port-side of the Squadron at 21,000 ft in a Westerly direction in the Alencon area.   I saw 3 e/a flying slightly below Eastwards.   Red section started diving and chasing them.   I turned with my section trying to catch them as well and lost sight of 2 of the e/a. I closed on the first e/a and gave him a burst with full deflection and was obliged to dive to avoid collision with him. I pulled up and came back again on a dive. I saw hits on this e/a from Red 1 and the hood flew off so I left Red 1 chasing him. Then flying alone I saw 15 Me 109's at 2,000 or 3,000 ft above me and announced by R/T "Bandits at 2 o'clock and above" Unfortunately I did not get any answer. Suddenly I saw an Me 109 diving steeply at approximately 15,000 ft coming from my starboard side. I got behind him and fired from 800 yards a 1 second burst with Cannon and M.G. dead astern. I was closing in but the e/a started an aileron turn which I followed. He pulled up at 3 or 4 thousand feet still diving. Closing on him I fired again dead astern from 600 yards to 200 yards with Cannon and M.G. I saw black smoke pouring out, the hood flew off and the pilot baled out. I had to pull up to avoid collision with the pilotless aircraft. Afterwards I saw the pilot hanging on his parachute. The e/a hit the ground in the middle of a wood and burst into flames. I kept diving and took photos of the e/a on the ground. Unfortunately my camera gun was u/s.
F/Sgt Moureau, Yellow 3 witnessed the combat and the crash of the e/a.
I claim 1 Me 109 destroyed.

.... F/Lt.

.... F/O. (Intelligence
Officer)

after a Mosquito tipped it over with its wings. The bomb started to burn less than fifteen yards from a Spitfire with full tanks. The mechanics dragged it to safety but the aircraft was a total write-off from the blast. Surprisingly, despite some minor damage to another Spitfire, only one person was slightly injured. During this first week 349 flew its ops as usual but, two days after the V-1 incident, it moved back to Selsey where ops remained unchanged, escorts with some sweeps between two Ramrods. On 18 August the squadron operated from the continent for the first time, carrying out two sweeps from B.10 before returning home. The unit moved again on 20 August, this time to Tangmere. It stayed there less than a week while preparing to move to the continent on the 30th after a couple of postponements. The ground party was flown to B.17/Caen-Carpiquet as early as 26 August. In the meantime, the pilots continued to operate from Tangmere. Sadly, on the 30th, while on a sweep over the Scheldt-Lys area south of Gant, ground targets were strafed and F/O M. Renard posted missing. He was last heard saying he was heading home and that his engine was overheating. While he was unable to reach Allied lines, he managed to evade capture. The next day, 349 began its operations from France for 2TAF. From then on, the nature of the squadron's tasks changed, focusing on Army support. The stay at Carpiquet was short as, to follow the rapid Allied advance, another move was made on 8 September, the new location being B.35/Le Tréport, then B.53/Merville on the 12th. Merville was home for the Belgians for the next six weeks. In September 349 flew more than 300 sorties but, while many ground targets were attacked and mostly destroyed, luck was with the squadron as no losses were suffered. In October, despite the autumnal weather gradually taking hold, 349 managed to log 340 sorties, claiming numerous targets destroyed or damaged on the ground. This time, however, the squadron sustained some losses. The first two occurred within two days. Flying Officer A. Vanderheyden was hit by flak near Gouda while attacking ground targets on the 5th. He was initially heard asking for a course home and later to say he was baling out; he evaded capture with the help of Dutch civilians and was back home on 22 October. The next day, while carrying out the second armed recce, this time near Amersfoort area in the Netherlands, some barges and METs were found and strafed, but W/O K.R. Brant (British) was hit by flak. He performed an emergency landing and initially evaded capture but was later taken prisoner west of Arnhem. Before Vanderheyden returned, the squadron experienced a very bad day on the 19th. In the morning support op, attacking the fort at Breskens, P/O C. de St-Aubin was lost to flak. On the return flight, his squadronmates heard him report over the radio that his oil pressure was zero, probably due to flak or gunfire damage. He tried to reach the Allied lines but had to fly low (about 1500 feet) and slow if he wanted to succeed. It was not enough. A few metres from the border of Belgium he crashed to his death in a field on the Zandstraat, probably after stalling too low to recover. In the afternoon, at approximately 16.00, S/L Van der Velde called on the R/T to say he had been hit by flak and was going down. From the little conversation that went on, he was unhurt and the pilots reported he was seen to land and get out of his aircraft. The CO was lucky as he crashed 200-300 yards from the front line defended by the Nova Scotia Highlanders of the Canadian Army. About a dozen soldiers came up to him and wanted to know why the aircraft was not marked with the usual black and white stripes on the wing. Van der Velde was able to convince them of his identity and was conveyed to the Battalion HQ time for tea. He was back with the squadron the next day. After a series of delays since 21 October, 349 moved to B.65/Maldeghem. The squadron operated from that base for the next two and a half months. The early days at Maldeghem were far from good, however, as the following day, after 349 dispatched aircraft in pairs to carry out armed recces in the Rheindahlen area, two pilots were posted missing – F/O H. Goldsmit and F/Sgt P. Decroix. Both were hit by flak when they entered a flak trap and both made an emergency landing. Decroix was later taken prisoner, but Goldsmit, who came down not far from the lines, managed to return. A few days later, on the 8th, another Spitfire was lost to flak while attacking ground targets near Dortrech. Flying Officer A. Uydens was hit over the target and was heard over the R/T to say his windscreen was damaged, but the engine still seemed to be running well and that he would make for base. The situation changed when he saw the coolant temperature rising rapidly and four minutes later reported he was crash landing within the Allied lines. He was seen to make a heavy landing; the aircraft turned over and one wing broke off. Flying Officer J. Croquet and F/Sgt J. Bragard stayed ten minutes, but Uydens was not seen to get out of the aircraft. Several civilians were seen in the vicinity and helped him get out before he was taken to a Canadian hospital. On 19 November, 349 only carried out one op to destroy a bridge and railway line near Amersfoort. The attack produced mixed results as, while the railway was cut, the bridge received no direct hits. Flak was as accurate as ever and hit the Spitfire flown by F/O M. Gendebien who was killed in the subsequent crash. Ten days later, Sgt R. Van Wymers was shot down and killed while attacking a German HQ near Dunkirk. November was a stand-out month for two reasons, neither of them positive; it was the most costly month with five Spitfire lost, two pilots killed and one taken PoW, and just 220 sorties were flown, the lowest total since D-Day. December reversed the trend with more than 280 sorties flown and only one loss reported (F/O M. Renard was killed on the 25th). Sent with eight other aircraft for a sweep near Saint-Vith for the second show of the day, Renard was seen returning from the attack, indicating a mechanical problem, and pointed downwards suggesting he was going to land. Sadly, he was killed in the crash.

Maldegem airfield was attacked by the Luftwaffe at around 09.20 on 1 January 1945 during Operation *Bodenplatte*. Considerable losses of aircraft were reported, but 349 was lucky and only one Spitfire was destroyed on the ground. The disturbance didn't last too long as 349 was airborne before midday for an armed recce on the Breda-Hertogenbosch road area. Armed recces were carried out as far as the weather permitted and about 180 were flown in January. A few major incidents were experienced, first on the 5th when F/O A. Vandenheyden and P/O R. Vandenbosch were forced to land after an attack on suspected German troop accommodation. Four more Spitfires were also hit, a good result considering this strongpoint was defended with effective small arms. Vandenbosch was forced to crash land between Geertruidenberg and Raamsdonksveer. His number two circled the crash site and waited until the pilot had left his aircraft, waving his arms to indicate he was uninjured. His Spitfire was later recovered and repaired, while Vandenheyden landed at B.77 with oil pressure trouble and was soon back at base. These were the only major events before the squadron moved to B.77/Gilze-Rigen in Holland on the 13th. Operations continued as usual from the new base but, one week later, an attack on several trains resulted in the loss of F/Sgt J. Leroy who was possibly hit by flak. He was heard over the target area to say he had engine trouble and was turning for base. As this occurred well within the enemy lines, he did not make it, crashed on the German side and was reported missing. He was eventually taken prisoner. Another Spitfire was also damaged when, short of petrol, it crash-landed in a field in the Allied lines. The pilot, F/Sgt J. Branders, was uninjured and the aircraft repairable. With the weather improving, more sorties were carried out in February, with 180 flown in the first half of the month, the same amount flown for all of January. On 3 February, twelve aircraft took off for an armed recce over the Gorinchem area. From this operation F/Sgt L. van de Werve was lost when his section went down to attack a lorry. It was partially obscured by trees and the pilots overshot on the first run so the section came in again. When looking around, no one could see van de Werve, nor could he be contacted on the R/T, but debris of an aircraft was seen and it was presumed he had hit the trees and not survived the crash. He was indeed killed. Three days later was another bad day for 349. The second operation of the day proved exceptionally unlucky. Flight Lieutenant J. Mascaux crashed on take-off due to a mechanical failure. He could only remember seeing tree branches and oil or black smoke on his windscreen before he crashed on the airfield. He was taken to hospital with facial injuries but nothing too serious and the Spitfire was repaired. The rest of the formation continued, but F/Sgt J. Blair, one of the British pilots of the squadron, was shot down. When returning over Zwolle his Blue Section went down to attack a train. The flak was heavy and two minutes after making the attack he called on the R/T to say his engine temperature was high and that he would return direct to base. Three minutes later he again called saying he was okay but had force-landed and asked where he was. Blue 1 (F/L M. Mycroft - British) replied that the target was Zwolle, meaning to indicate he was in that area. His actual landing place was south-west of Zwolle. He was presumed to be unhurt and, having landed within the enemy lines, was taken prisoner soon after. A third Spitfire was also lost that day. Soon after landing on return from the third show, the Spitfire flown by F/O A. Vanderheyden caught fire; nothing could be done to save the aircraft, but the pilot was safe.

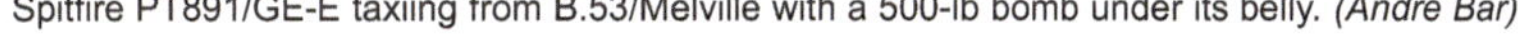

Spitfire PT891/GE-E taxiing from B.53/Melville with a 500-lb bomb under its belly. *(André Bar)*

Carpiquet, Normandy, end of summer 1944. Left to right: F/Sgt J. Leroy (PoW 22.01.45), possibly F/O J. Wood (British), possibly F/Sgt N. Leroy (J. Leroy's brother), P/O G. Halleux, F/Sgt J. Bragard, unknown, P/O A. Oger, F/Sgt A. Moureau, P/O R. Vandenbosch, S/L van de Velde, unknown, and F/O P. Erkes walking in front of PT385/GE-T.
Jean and Norbert Leroy were students in May 1940 who managed to flee Belgium for the USA where their parents were living. Later on, in January 1942, they both went to Canada to enlist in the RAF. They eventually joined together 349 Sqn in August 1944. Both survived the war, but Jean as a PoW. *(André Bar)*

On 13 February, 349 was ordered to move to Predannack in Cornwall to convert to the Hawker Tempest. The last sorties were carried out on the 16th and a few days later the squadron was at Predannack. Conversion to the Tempest started on the 24th but that was halted a few days later when the Tempests were sent to the continent, the RAF facing a shortage of the type with 2TAF. Some Typhoons arrived as replacements at the same time as the new CO, S/L R. Lallemant, a former Typhoon pilot with 609 Squadron who would officially take over at the end of March. The re-equipment soon proved a dead end. The squadron spent March and part of April flying Typhoons, only to be notified at the end that their return to the continent would be with Spitfires. Indeed, the squadron was re-assigned to 2TAF and placed under 132 (Norwegian) Wing authority which would provide their aircraft: Spitfire IXs! The personnel arrived at B.106/Twente, where 132 Wing was stationed, on 19 April and 349 was due to become operational on the 24th. That happened earlier as, on the 22nd, weather recces were carried out but the reports prevented any ops. The following day, however, thirty armed recces were flown even though ten aircraft returned early due to engine trouble. Operations continued on the 24th but one pilot was posted missing, F/L H. Wieck (British, on his second operational flight with the Belgians). When approximately eight miles south of Aurich, Wieck called on the R/T to say his engine was cutting out and he was about to make a forced landing. His number one turned around to search the locality but did not see him. He was eventually found safe. Luck was not on 349's side for long as, the day after, F/L A. Claessen was posted missing while attacking METs south of Wesermünde. He was last seen at treetop height making the attack. He was probably flying too low and hit the treetops and crashed. It was definitely not happy times for the Belgians as, two days later, another pilot lost his life. Flight Lieutenant J. Wood, a British pilot and the A Flight CO, was hit by flak while attacking METs near Lehmden, south of Varel. His aircraft caught fire and was seen crashing in flames. It was a deadly return to the continent for the squadron and somewhat bitter as the war's end was now so close. The following day, the 28th, 349 left 132 Wing to join 131 Wing. This unit was equipped with Spitfire XVIs so the squadron finally said goodbye to its Mk.IXs.

Date	Pilot	SN	Origin	Type	Serial	Code	Nb	Cat.
06.06.44	F/O Jean **Moreau de Melen**	RAF No. 138884	(BEL)/RAF	Ju88	**MK178**	GE-Q	0.5	C
	F/Sgt Joseph **Moureau**	RAF No. 1299855	(BEL)/RAF		**MK153**	GE-S	0.5	C
	F/Sgt Joseph **Van Molkot**	RAF No. 1814824	(BEL)/RAF	Ju88	**MK363**	GE-U	0.5	C
	Sgt Jean **Bragard**	RAF No. 1424828	(BEL)/RAF		**MJ955**	GE-T	0.5	C
08.06.44	F/L Gabriel **Seydel**	RAF No. 116541	(BEL)/RAF	Fw190	**MK354**	GE-V	1.5	C
	W/O Douglas F. **Clarke**	NZ417018	RNZAF		**MJ955**	GE-T	0.5	C
26.07.44	F/L Gabriel **Seydel**	RAF No. 116541	(BEL)/RAF	Bf109	**NH257**	GE-N	1.0	C
	F/L Paul **Siroux**	RAF No. 127853	(BEL)/RAF	Bf109	**ML404**	GE-E	1.0	C
28.07.44	F/O Jean **Moreau de Melen**	RAF No. 138884	(BEL)/RAF	*V-1*	**NH464**	GE-R	1.0	C

Total: 6.0 + 1 V-1

Among the Belgian pilots who scored while serving with 349 Sqn, the most successful was F/L G. Seydel (top left). He enlisted in the Belgian Aéronautique Militaire (AM) in September 1939 for a two-year contract and was still under training when he was evacuated with his Flying School to France then to the UK. He completed his training there and joined No. 131 Squadron in the summer of 1941 where a Belgian Flight had been raised, a flight that would become the nucleus of No. 350 (Belgian) Squadron. He completed his first tour in January 1943 and, by the end of the war, had completed another two tours with the Belgian squadrons as a flight CO. He survived the war with a DFC awarded in December 1945.

Middle, F/L P. Siroux, another flight commander, and another former NCO with the AM, was one of the few Belgians to fly the Hurricane operationally at the time. He became a PoW at the end of the campaign but was released in August 1940. He fled to the UK via Spain in October 1940 and was imprisoned for many months in Spain before being liberated and arriving in Gibraltar in January 1942. He joined the RAF and was re-trained and posted to No. 350 Squadron in January 1943, then to 349 Sqn until the end of his tour in February 1945. He survived the war and was awarded the DFC in July 1945.

F/O J. Moreau de Melen (top right) was another former pilot of the AM, an NCO newly posted to fly Fiat CR.42s when the Germans launched their offensive. He managed to avoid capture and left Belgium for the UK in November 1940, passing through Switzerland, unoccupied France and North Africa. He was arrested and spent a few months in prison before being liberated on parole in December 1941; he stayed in Morocco until the arrival of US troops in November 1942. Joining the RAF, he re-trained and joined 349 Sqn on its formation in June 1943. He served with the unit until the end of his tour in September 1944. He survived the war but held no further operational positions before the end of the war.

(André Bar)

Date	Pilot	S/N	Origin	Serial	Code	Fate
21.04.44	F/O Jean **Moreau de Melen**	RAF No. 138884	(BEL)/RAF	**MJ962**	GE-F	-
28.04.44	F/Sgt Henri **Limet**	RAF No. 1299911	(BEL)/RAF	**MH610**	GE-Z	**PoW**
10.05.44	F/O Paul **Libert**	RAF No. 161343	(BEL)/RAF	**MH491**		**PoW**
21.05.44	F/O Marcel **Sans**	RAF No. 138840	(BEL)/RAF	**MK192**	GE-H	-
28.05.44	F/O Jean **Ester**	RAF No. 127452	(BEL)/RAF	**MK130**	GE-P	-
06.06.44	F/Sgt Joseph **Van Molkot**	RAF No. 1814824	(BEL)/RAF	**MK363**	GE-U	**PoW***
07.06.44	F/O Marcel **Sans**	RAF No. 138840	(BEL)/RAF	**MJ748**	GE-A	†
08.06.44	F/Sgt Jean **Gheyssens**	RAF No. 1814842	(BEL)/RAF	**MK252**	GE-F	†
12.06.44	F/Sgt René **Vandenbosh**	RAF No. 1814841	(BEL)/RAF	**MK175**	GE-B	-
04.08.44	*Destroyed on the ground by a V-1*	-	-	**NH354**	GE-T	-
30.08.44	F/O Maurice **Renard**	RAF No. 159219	(BEL)/RAF	**NH199**	GE-J	-
05.10.44	F/O André **Vanderheyden**	RAF No. 162801	(BEL)/RAF	**PT730**	GE-R	**Eva.**
06.10.44	W/O Kenneth R. **Brant**	RAF No. 1575979	RAF	**PT395**		**PoW**
19.10.44	F/O Camille **de Saint Aubin**	RAF No. 130771	(BEL)/RAF	**PT841**	GE-R	†
	S/L Albert **Van de Velde**	RAF No. 123067	(BEL)/RAF	**PT555**	GE-M	-
03.11.44	F/O Henri **Goldsmit**	RAF No. 151928	(BEL)/RAF	**PT963**	GE-N	†
	F/Sgt Paul **Decroix**	RAF No. 1424878	(BEL)/RAF	**PV134**		**PoW**
08.11.44	F/O Alexander **Uydens**	RAF No. 153168	(BEL)/RAF	**PT891**	GE-E	**Inj.**
19.11.44	F/O Marc **Gendebien**	RAF No. 153365	(BEL)/RAF	**NH241**		†
29.11.44	F/Sgt Raymond **Van Wymers**	RAF No. 1424894	(BEL)/RAF	**RK838**		†
25.12.44	F/O Maurice **Renard**	RAF No. 159219	(BEL)/RAF	**RK802**	GE-Q	†
01.01.45	*Destroyed in air raid*	-	-	**PT830**	GE-X	-
22.01.45	F/Sgt Jean **Leroy**	RAF No. 1424886	(BEL)/RAF	**PL246**	GE-M	**PoW**
03.02.45	F/Sgt Léon **van de Werde de Vorsellaer**	RAF No. 1424855	(BEL)/RAF	**PT549**		†
06.02.45	F/Sgt Donald **Blair**	RAF No. 742018	RAF	**TA837**	GE-S	**PoW**
	F/O André **Vanderheyden**	RAF No. 162801	(BEL)/RAF	**PT946**	GE-T	-
24.04.45	F/L Hubert F. **Wieck**	RAF No. 126983	RAF	**PV185**		**PoW**
25.04.45	F/L Antoon **Claesen**	RAF No. 125846	(BEL)/RAF	**NH488**	GE-W	†
27.04.45	F/L John **Wood**	RAF No. 139514	RAF	**MK830**	GE-X	†

Total: 29

**Liberated by US troops in August*

Two pilots who did not make it. Left, F/Sgt R. van Wymers, a former cavalryman with the Belgian Army. He managed to flee to Cali in Colombia in May 1940 and avoid capture. He was eventually re-mobilised in October 1941 and later enlisted in the RAF. Trained as a pilot, he joined 349 Sqn in September 1944 and was killed two months later.
A few days before, F/O M. Gendebien was also killed in action. Another cavalryman in the reserve, he was made a PoW in May 1940. Liberated in June, he left Belgium in May 1941 and reached Gibraltar in January 1942 after some time in prison in Spain. He enlisted in the RAF in May and upon completing his training was posted to 349 Sqn in May 1944.
(André Bar)

Date	Pilot	S/N	Origin	Serial	Code	Fate
15.04.44	F/Sgt René **VANDENBOSH**	RAF No. 1814841	(BEL)/RAF	**MK136**	GE-N	-
29.04.44	F/Sgt Alfred **MOUREAU**	RAF No. 1299851	(BEL)/RAF	**MJ296**	GE-C	-
12.07.44	F/O Arthur A.G. **PATINY**	RAF No. 153064	RAF	**NH464**		†

Total: 3

Talking below the spinner of a Spitfire Mk.IX are, left to right, Sgt Alfred 'Freddy' Moureau, and Flight Sergeants J. Bragard and G. Halleux, the latter had served with 349 Sqn in Western Africa. Bragard was living in the Belgian Congo when war broke out and initially volunteered to serve in the 2nd Battalion *Transvaal Scottish* in August 1940 before joining the Belgian forces in the UK.

Below, Sgt Joseph Moureau, Alfred's twin brother. Both arrived in the UK in May 1940 as refugees. They enrolled in the RAF in October and were trained together as fighter pilots. They both arrived at 349 Sqn in July 1943, but didn't complete their tour at the same time, Joseph having had an unrelated aviation ground accident in June 1944, which took him away from ops until the end of the war, while Alfred finished his tour in February 1945. Both survived the war and worked for the Belgian airline SABENA. Even though not encouraged, it was not unusual in the RAF to have twin brothers serving in the same unit at the same time. *(André Bar - both)*

On readiness, left to right: F/Sgt J. Gheyssens (†08.06.44), Flying Officers J. Fromont, P. Libert (a former NCO pilot wounded on 10 May 1940 during the bombardment of Schaffen airfield), H. Taymans (†28.11.44), and H. Goldsmit (†03.11.44), P/O H. Bailly (a former Fairey Fox pilot shot down on 15 May 1940), F/L J. Morai, P/O G. Halleux, F/O J. Ester (previously with No. 350 Squadron, shot down on 16 June 1942, imprisoned by the French, then the Italians, before being liberated on parole in April 1943), F/L G. Seydel, and Flight Sergeants H. Limet and J. Moureau.

Together at Miranda in Spain, where they were held and escaped together, and together again with 350 Sqn. Now both flight commanders with 349 Sqn: Lucien Lelarge (in cockpit) and Paul Siroux.
(André Bar - both)

Above, some pilots during the winter of 1944-1945.
Front, left to right: Sgt J-P. Lacoste, F/O J. Croquet, S/L A. van de Velde (the CO), and F/L A. Claesen (†25.04.45). Claesen was an experienced pilot who had previously served with Nos. 350 and 232 Squadrons. When he joined 349 Sqn in January 1945, it was his second tour. Top: Flight Sergeants H. Branders and D. Blair (British, PoW 06.02.45), W/O D. A. Smerdon (British), F/L J. Wood (British, †27.04.45), F/Sgt L. van de Werve (†03.02.45), and F/O L. Paulis (IO).

Left, rest time for three 349 Sqn pilots. Left to right, F/L M.J. Mycroft, a British pilot who joined 349 in June 1944. He was awarded the DFC in September 1945 for his service with the squadron. In the middle, F/Sgt F. Pax joined in April 1945. A Belgian living in the UK when war broke out, he joined the Belgian forces in February 1941 but was transferred to become a pilot in September 1942. It was his first operational posting. On the right is F/O J. Croquet who completed two tours with 349. As with many of the Belgians of the unit, he was a former *Aéronautique Militaire* pilot (Fairey Fox) and veteran of the May-June 1940 campaign. He fled Belgium in March 1941 and arrived in the UK in January 1942, having crossed France, Spain, Portugal and Gibraltar to do so. *(André Bar - both)*

Victories - confirmed or probable claims: *nil*

First operational sortie:
06.01.44
Last operational sortie:
09.08.44

Number of sorties: *ca.* **800**

Total aircraft written-off: 4

Aircraft lost on operations: 2
Aircraft lost in accidents: 2

Squadron code letters:
MN

COMMANDING OFFICERS

S/L Adolphe Boussa	RAF No. 101465	(BEL)/RAF	...	06.01.44
S/L Léon Prévot	RAF No. 84285	(BEL)/RAF	06.01.44	...
S/L Michel Donnet	RAF No. 102522	(BEL)/RAF	...	...

Squadron Usage

After almost two years flying the Spitfire Mk.V (see *SQUADRONS! 30*), 350 Squadron began its transition to the Mk.IX in December 1943. At the time, the squadron was commanded by S/L A. Boussa and based at Hawkinge. On 30 December the squadron moved to Hornchurch where it took charge of the Spitfire Mk.IXs previously flown by No. 222 (Natal) Squadron. The pilots used the beginning of January 1944 to master their new mounts and carried out their first Spitfire IX sorties on the 6th with a Ranger of four aircraft, over Occupied Belgium around midday, followed by another a bit later. The sector chosen was Renaix-Courtrai and Tournai. A short skirmish occurred between the first section and Fw190s, but the Germans were quick to leave the area, while the second section flew an uneventful sortie. The same day, S/L Boussa ended his tour of operations and was replaced by S/L L. Prevot.

Over the next two days, 350 flew one sweep and two Ramrods (Nos. 431 and 440). Nothing else was flown until the 21st, but regular flying resumed from then until the end of the month. In all, eight Ramrods and two Rangers were flown during that period of time.

Léon Prévot joined the Belgian *Aéronautique Militaire* as an NCO in May 1934. In 1939 he was serving as a flying instructor. He was commissioned in February 1940 and in May was serving with the flying school with which he fled to France, then French Morocco, and eventually arrived in Great Britain in August 1940. He joined the RAF upon his arrival. He was re-trained and posted to No. 235 Squadron to fly Blenheims. In December he left to instruct French-Belgians at Odiham. In August 1941, after a refresher course at No. 58 OTU on Spitfires, he was posted to No. 123 Squadron, but, soon afterwards, was posted to No. 64 Squadron as a flight commander. He was given command of No. 122 (Bombay) Squadron in May 1942 but was shot down over France on 30 July only to evade capture with the help of the French Resistance and return to England in mid-October. The next month he was awarded the DFC shortly after being posted to No. 65 Squadron. He only stayed there for two weeks as he was posted to No. 197 Squadron as its first OC flying Typhoons. He remained with 197 until June 1943 when he was posted out for a rest. Six months later he returned to operations by assuming command of No. 350 Squadron. In March 1944, promoted to wing commander, he left 350 and served in various HQ positions until the end of war. Serving with the Belgian Air Force post-war, he retired in January 1964.
(André Bar)

Four Belgian pilots posing in front of a Spitfire IX.
Left to right, F/L L. Collignon (flight CO at the time, he would later command 350 Sqn in the autumn of 1944 before being severely wounded in action in December 1944), Flying Officers J. Lavigne and P. Siroux (he was later posted to 349 Sqn), and P/O J. Wustefeld. *(André Bar)*

All were uneventful until the Rangers were carried out. January 30 started badly when Ramrod 499 was cancelled due to bad weather. They were replaced by two Rangers (Nos. 7 and 8) in the afternoon. The first section, led by F/L L. Collignon, crossed the French coast near Nieuport and headed to Tournai where some barges were strafed near Saint-Omer. Not far from there, buildings were also strafed, as were gun posts near Calais, but, while doing so, F/O G. Duchesne, who was flying number two to Collignon, was shot down by flak. The aircraft crashed near Sainte-Marie-Kerke with Duchesne still on board. The second section, led by F/L R. Alexandre, didn't have any better luck as the formation was caught by flak heading to Saint-Pol-sur-Ternoise. Flying Officer J. Gérard was hit and obliged to leave the formation, heading home with a badly damaged Spitfire accompanied by P/O F. Verpoorten. While landing at Hawkinge, however, Gérard stalled, crashed and the Spitfire caught fire. Sadly, he did not survive. During the first week of February, 350 flew three uneventful Ramrods before it was sent on a ten-day Air Firing Course at Llanbedr. Returning to Hawkinge on the 20th, operations resumed on the 22nd with Ramrod 577. The squadron participated in six more Ramrods before the end of February. All were uneventful. In March, the unit continued its escort work, six being flown in the first week before a move to Scotland left the Spitfire IXs behind and the 350 returned to flying the Mk.V. During this first phase of the Mk.IX, 350 recorded about 330 sorties on the type.

The squadron continued to fly the Spitfire Mk.V well after D-Day and became one of the last to use the variant operationally. It was time to switch to a variant with more performance and 350 was notified early in July that it would re-equip with the Mk.IX again over the next few days. Of course, no transition period was needed and, having flown its last Spitfire V sorties on 4 July, the squadron carried out its first Mk.IX sorties on the 6th. By that time, 350 was still under ADGB authority and was based at Westhampnett under the leadership of S/L M. Donnet who had taken over in March. In July convoy patrols made up the majority of operational

'Mike' Donnet enlisted in the pre-war Belgian military forces to become a pilot. In May 1940 he was flying the Renard R.31, a Belgian co-operation aircraft, with the Army. He was made a PoW on 28 May and sent to Germany but was released in January 1941. He returned to Belgium but fled to Great Britain in July in an SV-4 biplane that had been hidden on the property of one of his friends. Upon arrival in England, he enlisted in the RAF, was re-trained and, in September, joined No. 64 Squadron. One year later, in September 1942, he became a flight commander and then the OC in March 1943. He had been awarded the DFC the previous January. His first tour ended in November and he returned to operations in March 1944 as OC of No. 350 (Belgian) Squadron, leading this unit until October when he became WingCo Flying of the Hornchurch Wing. He led the Mustang-equipped Bentwaters Wing in the same role from February 1945. Donnet, therefore, became one the very few Belgian pilots to fly Mustangs operationally during the war. He left the Wing in August and was discharged from the RAF in October 1946. Continuing his career in the new Belgian Air Force, he reached the rank of Lieutenant-General and retired in 1975. *(André Bar)*

sorties, but some Ramrods were carried out over Normandy. More than 300 sorties were flown in July, all being uneventful. Despite this, 350 was not spared drama. This second association with the Mk.IX was marred by the death of a British pilot as early as the 8th. Five Spitfires had taken off for formation practice that day when white smoke, coming from the right side of the cowling of the Spitfire flown by Sgt J. Wooley, was seen by F/O R. Duchâteau just before a round object flew off the left side followed by an explosion. Before disintegrating, the Spitfire became a mass of fire from the nose to tail. Wooley had no time to bale out. An engine failure was the cause of the loss of another Spitfire five days later, once more during a practice flight. Unable to re-start his engine, F/O P. Delorme crashed the aircraft on the edge of the aerodrome. While levelling out, he struck an anti-glider obstruction and overturned. The Spitfire was only good for scrap, but the pilot escaped with slight injuries. In August, news was received that 350 Squadron would participate in the anti-diver campaign and would re-equip with the Griffon-engine Spitfire XIV (see SQUADRONS! 37). The squadron continued to fly ops in the first week of August, close to 150 sorties being flown that week. On the evening of the 8th, the unit moved back to Hawkinge where it flew its last Spitfire IX ops the next day, an escort of Bostons to the Rouen area. Then, 350 opened a new chapter with its new Spitfire XIVs. It was now set for a much more intense and successful period of operations.

Summary of the aircraft lost on Operations - 350 Squadron

Date	Pilot	S/N	Origin	Serial	Code	Fate
30.01.44	P/O Georges **DUCHENE**	RAF No. 132975	(BEL)/RAF	**MH428**	MN-Z	†
	F/O Jean **GÉRARD**	RAF No. 132971	(BEL)/RAF	**MH476**	MN-F	†
			Total: 2			

Summary of the aircraft lost by accident - 350 Squadron

Date	Pilot	S/N	Origin	Serial	Code	Fate
08.07.44	Sgt Joseph F. **WOOLEY**	RAF No. 1578305	RAF	**MK123**		†
13.07.44	F/O Paul **DELORME**	RAF No. 157939	(BEL)/RAF	**MK301**		-
			Total: 2			

Spitfire ML137/MN-Z was the regular mount of F/L G. de Patoul who was at the end of his tour in July 1944; he was serving 350 since September 1942. He would return to 350 in April 1945 and shot down soon after on the 24th to spend the last days of the war as a PoW. The aircraft had the standard markings of the time although the spinner had the Belgian roundel painted on it. (André Bar)

Victories - confirmed or probable claims: *Nil*

Number of sorties: *ca.* **600**

First operational sortie:
11.08.44
Last operational sortie:
07.10.44

Total aircraft written-off: 9

Aircraft lost on operations: 8
Aircraft lost in accidents: 1

Squadron code letters:

3W

COMMANDING OFFICERS

Maj Keith C. KUHLMANN *(PoW)*	SAAF No. P102441	SAAF	...	01.09.44
S/L Leendert C.M. VAN EENDENBURG	RAF No. 108814	(NL)/RAF	12.09.44	...

SQUADRON USAGE

After having participated in the V-1 hunt with its Spitfire XIVs (see *SQUADRONS! 37*), 322 Squadron was tasked with a new role in August 1944 and returned to the Ramrods (escorts) it had flown while flying the Spitfire Mk.V (see SQUADRONS! 30). The squadron was, at the time, led by a South African, Major K.C. Kuhlmann, who had been in charge for about a year. It was with much regret that the exchange of aircraft took place at Hawkinge on 9 August. Unfortunately, in returning to 322's base, Deanland, Flying Officer A. Homburg crashed on landing; his Spitfire caught fire, but he managed to get out safely despite receiving first degree burns to his hand that required treatment at hospital. This was far from a good start for the unit's association with the Mk.IX, but what would follow would be even more dramatic! The next two days were spent preparing the machines for the next escort which eventually took place on the 11th. The Dutch were still working with No. 91 Squadron which had also just traded its Spitfire XIVs for IXs. The first escort was, as mentioned, carried out on the 11th, covering 120 Lancasters targeting marshalling yards at Douai (Ramrod 1186), the two squadrons taking care of the rear half of the bomber formation. The wing leader, W/C R.X. Oxspring, flew with 322 on this occasion. Later that day, ten Halifaxes heading to bomb

'Kees' van Eendenburg was born in the Netherlands East Indies. When war broke out, he was still a student in the Netherlands, while serving as a reserve artillery officer in the Dutch Army. In May 1940, the country was occupied and out of the war in five days. He managed to escape to England in July 1940. First enlisting in the Royal Navy in August 1940, he was transferred to the RAF in February 1941, completed his training and, in December 1941, was posted to No. 41 Squadron. He made his first claim, an Fw190 destroyed, on 3 May 1942 but was posted to No. 167 Squadron in July. This unit had one of its two flights manned by Dutch aircrew. He remained with 167 until May 1943 during which he added one shared confirmed victory. In June 1943, the flight was raised to full squadron strength and became No. 322 (Dutch) Squadron. He became one of its flight commanders in February 1944, a position he held until being promoted OC in September, relinquishing command in November. He was then posted to HQFC but continued to fly operationally from time to time. He was transferred to the new RNethAF in February 1946 and retired two years later.

Wearing the Dutch orange triangle under the cockpit, Spitfire Mk.IX MJ360/3W-K receives some final attention from the groundcrew before its next flight. Note the Spitfire's underside which was prone to weathering and staining from oil leaks, mud and dust. The invasion stripes, which were often hastily and crudely applied, had a rough surface on which such weathering appeared much faster than on the parts of the fuselage where the factory-applied, spray-painted paint coat was much smoother. This explains that on many photos the invasion stripes appear completely black on the parts of the fuselage most exposed to weathering. (see also ML137 of 350 Sqn p24)

a Noball target (V-weapon sites) in France were also escorted (Ramrod 1188). Both ops were uneventful. The next day, however, a tragic event occurred. On another escort (Ramrod 1190), F/O J. Jonker developed engine trouble and was obliged to turn for home, escorted by F/O R. Burgwal. He landed safely at Rennes aerodrome (the fate of the Spitfire remains unclear) but lost touch with Burgwal who was reported missing. He was the top V-1 scorer of the squadron, and therefore top Dutch scorer, with nineteen claimed destroyed. Escorts continued until the end of the month, the squadron flying almost every day, sometimes three times a day. From the 23rd onwards, some Rodeos were carried out alongside the regular escorts and several armed recces. This gave the Dutch the chance to attack some targets of opportunity. These were more dangerous than simple escorts, however, and while strafing some METs during an armed recce in the Calais-Aulnoye-Ghent area, F/Sgt R. van Beers developed engine trouble, possibly hit by ground fire, and turned for home. His engine soon failed, so he told F/Sgt J. Harms, who had accompanied him, he would bale out over the Channel. A few days later, on the 30th, and in the same area, it was the turn of F/O M. Muller to be hit by flak. He was heard to say he was baling out and was eventually posted missing. Fortunately, he managed to evade capture and was back with the squadron on 11 September. The last day of August consisted of one Ramrod (No 1250) and an armed recce, both uneventful, for a total of 320 sorties for the month, but at a cost of four Spitfires and two pilots lost. Even during the Spitfire XIV era, 322 had not known such losses. Worse was yet to come. On 1 September the squadron took off at 07.12 for an armed reconnaissance over the usual Calais-Ghent-Aulnoye area; four METs and one light AFV were destroyed. Another MET and AFV were also damaged. While going down to shoot up something he had seen, the CO, Major Kuhlmann, was apparently hit by flak and had to bale out about five miles inland near Cap Griz-Nez. His number two saw him land and wave. He was captured soon after. The squadron returned without its CO and took off again at 10.27 for another armed reconnaissance in the same area; this time a gun post was attacked and two METs damaged. The flak was very accurate once more; this time F/L L. van Eendenburg, the A Flight CO, was hit and made a forced landing south-east of Lille, while F/L J. Plesman, the B Flight CO, had his tail shot off. He was seen to spin in north-east of Saint-Omer. He was not seen leaving his aircraft and was indeed killed in the subsequent crash. Van Eendenburg's luck held and he managed to evade capture to return to England eleven days later. In a single day, the squadron had lost its CO and two flight commanders, a severe blow for the Dutch who were already suffering a shortage of leaders and pilots for their flying units. Severe gales over the next few days prevented operational flying. This gave the squadron time to recover from the loss of its leaders and appoint replacements. As an immediate measure, command was given to F/L W. de Wolff (the new A Flight CO), but soon after temporary command was transferred to F/L J. van Arkel (the new B Flight CO) who held the position until a new CO was appointed. When, on 12 September, F/L van Eendenburg returned to 322 after his escape, he assumed command. In the meantime, operations resumed and it soon became obvious the period of bad luck had yet to run its course. On 16 September, the squadron was called to participate in a late afternoon armed recce over the The Hague-Den Helder-Amsterdam-Utrecht. Shortly after take-off Flying Officers C. Manders and D. Wolters collided while climbing through cloud in line astern. Wolters crashed near Hawkinge and was killed while Manders baled out and landed safely. Despite this, the squadron continued its armed recce and escort work and soon had its first encounter with the Luftwaffe while escorting glider-towing Dakotas over Holland during Operation Market. Patrolling the Eindhoven area, Flying Officers P. Cramerus and G. Jongbloed spotted enemy aircraft attacking a returning Dakota. Cramerus reported to the wing leader (W/C Oxspring) who ordered the formation to drop its auxiliary fuel tanks. An attack followed at once. Cramerus engaged the Fw190 attacking the Dakota, closed in and fired a short burst of cannon and machine guns from about 200 yards; no results were observed. The Fw190 rolled on its back at which time Cramerus got him in his sight again. He fired another, longer, burst of two seconds and saw strikes on the wing roots and fuselage. The Fw190 dived and was last seen entering cloud at 4000 feet in a vertical dive. It was claimed as damaged while F/O Jongbloed claimed another Fw190 as damaged. The Dutch went back over the bridges as cover for Operation *Market* and then returned to its conventional escort duties, but the rest of the month proved uneventful. At the beginning of October, the pilots were advised they were going to attend a course on bombing, and air-to-ground and air-to-air firing, meaning the squadron's role would change to close air support. The course was scheduled to be held at Fairwood Common from the 10th. Therefore, the squadron was stood down, but a last op, Ramrod 1319, an escort for Halifaxes bombing Cleves, was carried out on the 7th. In the middle of the course, personnel were notified that, as the course was completed, the squadron would re-equip with Spitfire XVIs (more suitable for the new tasks to be carried out). At the end of October, 322 moved to Biggin Hill and, on the 4th, an exchange of machines was made, the pilots trading their Spitfire IXs for brand new XVIs at 84 GSU. This exchange ended a somewhat painful association between the Dutch and the Spitfire IX.

Summary of the aircraft lost on Operations - 322 Squadron

Date	Pilot	S/N	Origin	Serial	Code	Fate
12.08.44	F/O Rudolph F. **Burgwal**	RAF No. 113893	(NL)/RAF	**MH370**	3W-L	†
26.08.44	F/Sgt Ronald L. **van Beers**	RAF No. 1814965	(NL)/RAF	**MJ232**	3W-C	**PoW**
30.08.44	F/O Martin A. **Muller**	RAF No. 135760	(NL)/RAF	**MK684**	3W-V	**Eva.**
01.09.44	Maj Keith C. **Kuhlmann**	SAAF No. P102441	SAAF	**MK905**	3W-G	**PoW**
	F/L Leendert C.M. **van Eendenburg**	RAF No. 108814	(NL)/RAF	**PL238**	3W-E	**Eva.**
	F/L Jan L. **Plesman**	RAF No. 102524	(NL)/RAF	**MJ343**	3W-P	†
16.09.44	F/O Lambert D. **Wolters**	RAF No. 141896	(NL)/RAF	**MJ460**	3W-N	†
	F/O Coenraad R.R. **Manders**	RAF No. 113889	(NL)/RAF	**MK208**	3W-R	-

Total: 8

Successful on Spitfire XIVs against the V-1s, F/O R. Burgwal, on the left, was the first squadron loss a few days after No. 322 Squadron's conversion to the Mk.IX. About two weeks later, another successful V-1 hunter, F/L J. Plesman (right), was lost.

Summary of the aircraft lost by accident - 322 Squadron

Date	Pilot	S/N	Origin	Serial	Code	Fate
09.08.44	P/O Aart A. **Homburg**	RAF No.125169	(NL)/RAF	**MJ243**		-

Total: 1

IN MEMORIAM

Spitfire Mk IX - The Belgian and Dutch Squadrons

Name	Service No	Rank	Age	Origin	Date	Serial
BURGWAL, Rudolph Frans	RAF No. 113893	F/O	26	(NL)/RAF	12.08.44	MH370
CLAESEN, Antoon Eliza Léon	RAF No. 125846	F/L	23	(BEL)/RAF	25.04.45	NH488
DE **SAINT-AUBIN**, Camille Albert J.G.	RAF No. 130771	F/O	26	(BEL)/RAF	19.10.44	PT841
DUCHENE, Georges François Jean	RAF No. 132975	P/O	27	(BEL)/RAF	30.01.44	MH428
GENDEBIEN, Marc Maurice L.M.J.G.	RAF No. 153365	F/O	32	(BEL)/RAF	19.11.44	NH241
GÉRARD, Jean Jules Victor	RAF No. 132971	F/O	34	(BEL)/RAF	30.01.44	MH476
GHEYSSENS, Jean Louis Marie Pierre	RAF No. 1814824	F/Sgt	28	(BEL)/RAF	08.06.44	MK252
GOLDSMIT, Henri Maurice	RAF No. 151928	F/O	28	(BEL)/RAF	03.11.44	PT963
PLESMAN, Jan Leendert	RAF No. 102524	F/L	24	(NL)/RAF	01.09.44	MJ343
RENARD, Maurice Célestin Bernard	RAF No. 159219	F/O	30	(BEL)/RAF	25.12.44	RK802
SANS, Marcel Adrien	RAF No. 138840	F/O	29	(BEL)/RAF	07.06.44	MJ748
VAN DE **WERVE DE VORSELLAER**, Léon A.M.J.G.	RAF No. 1424855	F/Sgt	23	(BEL)/RAF	03.02.45	PT549
VAN WYMERS, Raymond	RAF No. 1424894	F/Sgt	32	(BEL)/RAF	29.11.44	RK838
WOOD, John	RAF No. 139514	F/L	*n/k*	RAF	27.04.45	MK830
WOOLEY, Joseph Francis	RAF No. 15780305	Sgt	21	RAF	08.07.44	MK123
WOLTERS, Lambertus Douwes	RAF No. 141896	F/O	24	(NL)/RAF	16.09.44	MJ460

Total: 16

Belgium: 11, Netherlands: 3, UK: 2

Left, F/O C. de Saint-Aubin served for about two months with 349 Sqn before he was killed in action in October 1944. A former Belgian cavalryman in May 1940, he was captured, then liberated in December 1940, and left Belgium one year later, reaching the UK in July 1942. The squadron was his first operational position after serving as a flying instructor.

Right, P/O G. Duchesne of 350 Sqn. A former Belgian pilot on Renard R.31s, a co-operation aircraft, he was injured on 14 May and became a PoW in hospital. Later released, he fled Belgium in March 1942 and reached the UK in August 1942 where he re-enlisted. He had been serving with 350 since April 1943 when he was killed in January 1944. *(André Bar)*

Supermarine Spitfire Mk.IX MK265
No. 322 (Dutch) Squadron
Squadron Leader Leendert van EENDENBURG (Dutch)
Hawkinge (UK), September 1944

Supermarine Spitfire Mk.IX MJ360
No. 322 (Dutch) Squadron
Deanland (UK), September 1944

Supermarine Spitfire Mk.IX MJ748
No. 349 (Belgian) Squadron
Selsey (UK), spring 1944

Supermarine Spitfire Mk.IX ML365
No. 349 (Belgian) Squadron
Squadron Leader Yvan du MONCEAU de BERGENDAL (Belgian)
Selsey (UK), June 1944

Supermarine Spitfire Mk.IX PT891
No. 349 (Belgian) Squadron
B.53/Merville (France), autumn 1944

Supermarine Spitfire Mk.IX ML137

No. 350 (Belgian) Squadron
Flight Lieutenant Guy de PATOUL (Belgian)
Westhampnett (UK), July 1944

SQUADRONS! - The series

Donald James Matthew BLAKESLEE DFC

Supermarine Spitfire Mk.VB EN951
No. 133 (Eagle) Squadron
Flight Lieutenant D. J. M. Blakeslee
RAF No. 41810
CAN./ J.4551
Gravesend (UK), August 1942

Charles Cuthbertson LEARMONTH DFC*

Douglas Boston Mk. III A28-9 (ex-AL811)
No. 22 Squadron RAAF
Squadron Leader C. C. Learmonth
A205
Port Moresby (New Guinea), spring 1943

Hans Anton MAURENBRECHER

Curtiss P-40N-35-CU C3-560
No. 120 (NEI) Squadron
Major H. Maurenbrecher
RAF No. 112709
Biak (New Guinea), 1943-1946

Roland Prosper BEAMONT DSO* DFC*

Hawker Tempest Mk. V JN751
No. 150 Wing
Wing Commander R. P. Beamont
RAF No. 41810
Bradwell Bay (UK), April 1944

Ronald Thomas SUSANS DSO DFC

North American P-51D-25-NT A68-724
No. 77 Squadron, RAAF
Squadron Leader R. T. Susans
O4391
Bofu (Japan), 1947

James Henry LACEY DFM*

Supermarine Spitfire Mk.XIV RN135
No. 17 Squadron
Squadron Leader J. H. Lacey
RAF No. 112709
Seletar (Singapore), autumn 1945

Introducing's RAF In Combat and Bravo Bravo Aviation's collection of
highly-detailed and historically accurate, high-quality aviation prints.
For more information on available prints, please visit :

www.RAF-IN-COMBAT.com   or

BRAVO BRAVO AVIATION
BBA
HIGH QUALITY AVIATION ILLUSTRATION
WWW.BravoBravoAviation.com

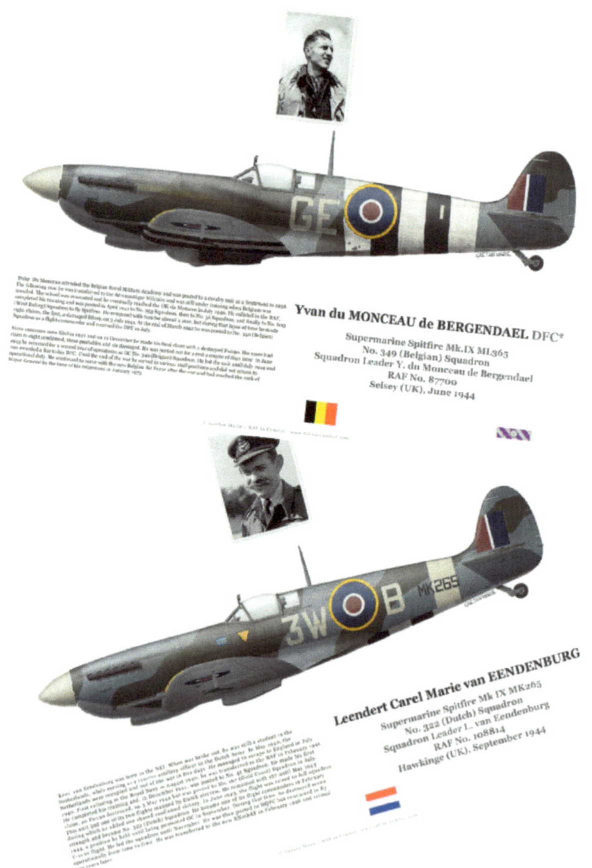

Yvan du MONCEAU de BERGENDAEL DFC*

Supermarine Spitfire Mk.IX ML265
No. 349 (Belgian) Squadron
Squadron Leader Y. du Monceau de Bergendael
RAF No. 87700
Selsey (UK), June 1944

Leendert Carel Marie van EENDENBURG

Supermarine Spitfire Mk IX MK265
No. 322 (Dutch) Squadron
Squadron Leader L. van Eendenburg
RAF No. 108814
Hawkinge (UK), September 1944

Prints available for this book:

PL-014: Y. du Monceau
PL-091: L. van Eendenburg